WHEN GOD TORE THE CURTAIN

Copyright © 2017 Basic Gospel, Inc., Lewisville, TX 75057
ISBN 978-1-931899-43-7

WHEN GOD TORE THE CURTAIN
The mystery that has been kept hidden for ages and generations!

Acknowledgments

Ted Clemens created the cover for **WHEN GOD TORE THE CURTAIN**. Ted and his wife, Becky, have been part of our Basic Gospel family for many years.

Kim Groff, who is on our staff, and Jeannie Thompson, now an active volunteer, wrote the text.

Chris Thompson, Jeannie's grandson, created the inside illustrations.

Greg Parke, Basic Gospel's radio producer, served as editor–producer for this book.

Michele Lister, a longtime staff member supervised the in–house printing.

Vivian Foster had the final say as our senior proofreader.

Other staff members who have given unlimited support and encouragement are Bob Davis, Richard Peifer, Billie Raybourn, Stephen Simon, and Coleman Christopher.

Bob Christopher's leadership of this New Covenant ministry of God's grace encourages all of us in the **Basic Gospel** family to "Keep our eyes on Jesus."

Contents

Life and Death in the Garden of Eden   7

The Man with Billions of Grandsons   13

Frogs, Frogs, and MORE FROGS!   17

Obedience – Mission Impossible!   23

A Temporary Tabernacle and Priesthood   27

Time for a Change - God Sends His Son   33

When God Tore the Curtain   39

What if there had been No Resurrection?   43

WHO is the Holy Spirit?   49

Have you Crossed Over to Eternal Life in Jesus?   53

Are You Ready for the Trip of a Lifetime?   57

Epilogue   62

How did he ever come up with duckbill platypus, orangutan, and hippopotamus?!

Adam really did name the animals. (Genesis 2:19-20)

Where and when did God's mystery begin?

Life and Death in the Garden of Eden
(John 1:1-4; Genesis 1:1-3:24)

God's Perfect World

It was the sixth day of Creation. God was almost finished making his perfect world. After creating the animals, he formed a man from the dust of the ground and breathed into him the breath of life. The man was created in the very image of God. Then, on the seventh day, God rested from his work.

God named the man Adam and placed him in the Garden of Eden, which he had created earlier, to "work it and take care of it."

Soon God gave Adam a command:

He said, *"You are free to eat from any tree in the garden; but you must not eat from the tree of the knowledge of good and evil, for when you eat of it you will surely die"* Genesis 2:16-17).

Adam and the animals must have really enjoyed living in this beautiful paradise! God even brought the animals to Adam so he could name them. Genesis 2:19-20

There were many creatures that Adam could enjoy and also use in caring for the garden, but God knew that Adam also needed a person to love and share his life. While Adam was sleeping, God created Eve from one of Adam's ribs to become his wife and companion.

There was still no sin in the garden or in the whole world, and what wonderful fellowship Adam and Eve enjoyed with the Lord. In the cool of the evening, God would even come to the garden and visit with them.

You and I would be enjoying life in the Garden of Eden or a similar paradise setting today if a tragic event had not occurred. You probably know what happened.

One day, the devil, in the form of a serpent appeared in the garden. He told Eve a terrible lie about God and the forbidden tree, and she believed him!

God's Perfect World – What Happened?

The serpent said to Eve, *"Did God really say, 'You must not eat from any tree in the garden?'"*

Eve replied, *"We may eat fruit from the trees in the garden, but God did say, 'You must not eat fruit from the tree that is in the middle of the garden (the tree of the knowledge of good and evil) and you must not touch it, or you will die.'"*

"You will not die," the serpent said to her. *"God knows that when you eat fruit from that tree your eyes will be opened, and you will be like God, knowing good and evil."*

When Eve saw that the fruit was good for food and pleasing to the eye, and also desirable for gaining wisdom, she took some and ate it. She also gave some to Adam, who was with her, and he ate it.

Adam and Eve had listened to the devil and had disobeyed God. They thought they were wiser than God. How wrong they were!

They both died, just as God had said they would if they ate fruit from the forbidden tree. They did not die physically, but they did die spiritually. Their spirits no longer were alive with the inner presence of God's Spirit. Sin had now invaded God's perfect world through Adam and Eve. They had to leave the Garden of Eden, which was no longer a garden paradise, but a garden of death.

Since that time, their sin nature has been passed down to you and me and to every person who has ever been born. Your body was alive at birth, but your spirit was already dead, because God's penalty for sin is death!

For the wages of sin is death, but the gift of God is eternal life in Christ Jesus our Lord (Romans 6:23).

There was no question about God's penalty for sin, but God promised that one day in the future he would send a Savior, his own Son Jesus, to die **in our place** for every sin – past, present and future. We would be forgiven forever!

Jesus, our Savior, has come! He died for all of our sins, and because he received eternal life through his resurrection, God gives eternal life to everyone who believes in his Son, and in his death, burial, and resurrection!

For just as through the disobedience of the one man (Adam) the many were made sinners, so also through the obedience of the one man (Jesus) the many will be made righteous (Romans 5:19).

When God Tore the Curtain

Does anyone have a spare donkey?

The Lord said to Abram (whom he later named Abraham)
"Leave your country, your people, and your father's household
and go to the land I will show you" (Genesis 12:1).

The Man with Billions of Grandsons
(Genesis 12:1-7; 15:1-6; 21:1-7; 22:1-19)

It was moving day for Abraham and Sarah, but there was one problem: They didn't know where they were moving! This was God's plan, and Abraham trusted God to guide them.

The Lord had said to Abraham (who was then known as Abram), *"Leave your own country, your people and your father's household and go to the land I will show you. I will make you into a great nation and I will bless you... and all people on earth will be blessed through you"* (Genesis 12:1-3).

The years passed, and in every situation Abraham trusted God. But when Abraham was about 99 years old and his wife, Sarah, was 89, they still had no children of their own. Without descendants, how would Abraham become the father of billions of grandsons? How would all the people on earth be blessed though him?

Abraham talked to God about his concern. It was nighttime, and God took Abraham outside and said: *"Look up at the heavens and count the stars, if indeed you can count them all. So shall your descendants be.*" Again Abraham believed God, and the very next year, when Abraham was 100 and Sarah, 90, little Isaac was born. God always keeps his word!

Oh, how Abraham loved his son! When Isaac was approaching "middle school" age, Abraham faced the greatest challenge of his life where trusting God was concerned. One day, God said to Abraham, *"Take your son Isaac to the region of Moriah. Sacrifice him there as a burnt offering on one of the mountains I will tell you about."*

This must have seemed like a very cruel command coming from a loving God! Some of the pagan religions of that day practiced human sacrifice, but not the true God and those who were led by him. Also, Isaac was the child of promise, Abraham and Sarah's only child. Had God changed His mind about Abraham becoming the Father of a great nation and blessing all nations? But again, Abraham trusted and obeyed God.

Early the next morning, Abraham got up and saddled his donkey. He cut enough wood for the burnt offering and then started the long journey to Moriah with two of his servants and Isaac.

On the third day, Abraham looked up and saw the mountain God had chosen as the location for the sacrifice. He said to his servants, *"Stay here with the donkey while Isaac and I continue up the mountain. We will worship and then come back to you."*

Abraham placed the pieces of wood on Isaac's back, and he himself carried the fire and the knife as they started up the mountain. At one point, Isaac looked up at Abraham and said, *"Father, the fire and wood are here, but where is the lamb for the burnt offering?"* Abraham replied, *"God himself will provide the lamb, my son."* And the two of them continued on together.

When they reached the place for the sacrifice, Abraham built an altar and arranged the wood on top. Then he bound Isaac and laid him on the altar on top of the wood. The time had come. Abraham raised his hand with the knife to slay his son.

But then he heard a voice calling out to him from heaven, *"Abraham! Abraham! Do not harm Isaac. Now I know you fear God for you have not withheld from me your son, your only son"* (Genesis 22:11-12).

At that moment, as Abraham looked toward a thicket, he saw a ram caught by its horns. Abraham knew the ram had been provided by the Lord. He brought the ram to the altar and sacrificed it for a burnt offering instead of his son. Then he heard this message from the Lord:

"Because you have not withheld your only son, whom you love, I will surely bless you and make your descendants as the stars in the sky and the sand on the seashore. Your descendants will take possession of the cities of their enemies, and through your offspring, all nations on earth will be blessed" (Genesis 22:15-19).

Romans 4:3 says, *"Abraham believed God, and it was credited to him as righteousness."* May it be the same with you and me.

The Lord said to Moses, "Go to Pharaoh and say to him, 'Let my people go, so that they may worship me. If you refuse to let them go, I will plague your whole country with frogs…'" (Exodus 8:1-3).

Frogs, Frogs, and MORE FROGS!
(Exodus 3:1-14:31)

Many years had passed. Isaac's son, Jacob, whose name was changed to "Israel", had become the father of twelve sons. The offspring of these sons had become known as the twelve *tribes* of Israel, and had now been slaves in Egypt over 400 years, suffering terrible persecution.

The twelve sons had originally lived in Canaan, the land God had given their great grandfather, Abraham. *How did they end up in Egypt?* You will learn the answer by reading the extraordinary story of Joseph, recorded in Genesis, Chapters 37-46:7.

These twelve tribes were God's chosen people. Although their path had not been an easy one, God had caused his people, also called Hebrews, to grow in strength and numbers during their bondage in Egypt. There were now about 600,000 Hebrew men over 20 years old, plus all their wives and children.

God was now ready to free the Hebrews so they could travel back to Canaan, the Promised Land. He called on Moses, who was then 80 years old, to lead his people on this journey, with the help of his brother Aaron, 83. God himself would be in front of the travelers as a pillar of cloud by day and a pillar of fire by night.

Getting Pharaoh, the ruler of Egypt, to release the Hebrew slaves would not be an easy task. He and the other Egyptians would not want to give up all of their free slave labor! God hardened Pharaoh's heart so that through a series of terrible plagues, pagan Egypt, along with their ruler, might finally realize that the God of Moses was the one true God; (Exodus 7:3-5).

God usually talked directly to Moses, who would then pass needed information on to Aaron. When Moses and Aaron first confronted Pharaoh, Moses, heeding God's instructions, told Aaron to throw down his shepherd's staff. As proof they had been sent by God, the staff turned into a snake. Pharaoh's wise men and magicians did the same thing with their staffs, but Aaron's snake gobbled up their snakes.

Pharaoh's heart was still hardened, so God sent the ten plagues to Egypt, one after the other, to get Pharaoh's attention and secure the release of Israel. These plagues were intended only for the Egyptians. The Hebrew slaves, God's people, were not affected by any of the plagues.

The Ten Plagues

Plague #1 – Every river and body of water was changed to blood; all the fish died. Even the drinking water became blood.

Plague #2 – Frogs came from the Nile into every Egyptian home, into the Egyptians' beds, their ovens and all over the people.

Plague #3 – Swarms of flies were all over Egypt and inside every Egyptian home.

Plague #4 – Egyptian horses, donkeys, camels, cattle, sheep, and goats died of a terrible plague.

Plague #5 – Festering boils broke out on Egyptian men and animals.

Plague #6 –The worst hailstorm of all time fell on Egypt. The hailstones killed any Egyptian or animal that happened to be outside.

Plague #7 – Locusts covered every inch of ground, every tree, and filled every Egyptian house.

Plague #8 – Total darkness covered Egypt for three days.

Plague #9 – The dust became gnats, and these gnats tortured every Egyptian and their animals.

Still Pharaoh refused to let the Hebrews leave Egypt with Moses and Aaron, so God sent the 10th and final plague.

Plague #10 – Every firstborn Egyptian son, including Pharaoh's own son, and the firstborn calves of the Egyptian cattle, died.

In preparation for this 10th plague, God gave the Hebrews instructions for a quick departure from Egypt. Each family was to prepare a lamb for their nighttime meal. Its blood was to be smeared on the top and sides of the door frame of each Hebrew house.

As God (or the angel of God) passed through Egypt to carry out this final plague of death, he would see the blood and *pass over* those homes belonging to the Hebrew families. The Hebrews and their descendants were told to celebrate Passover forever as a special festival to the Lord.

After midnight, many Egyptians were mourning the deaths of their firstborn sons. Pharaoh's own son was one of the dead. Pharaoh then begged Moses and Aaron to leave Egypt immediately with God's people and all of their livestock and possessions, as well as many additional possessions of the Egyptian people.

After 430 years in bondage as slaves, these 600,000 men, with all of their wives and children and animals, left Egypt and started on the long trek to Canaan. God had rescued his people out of slavery.

So the matter was settled – *or was it?* Not quite. Pharaoh and the Egyptian officials were still not ready to let Israel go; they had changed their minds! Pharaoh called out his troops to pursue the Hebrews, and he himself led the chase in his chariot. All the forces in Pharaoh's army - his horses, chariots, and charioteers – were used in the pursuit.

The Egyptians caught up with the people of Israel while they were camped near the shores of the Red Sea. When the Israelites realized they were being pursued, they were terrified and turned against Moses. "Why did you bring us out here to die in the wilderness? Weren't there enough graves for us in Egypt?!" And the complaints went on and on.

Then the Lord said to Moses, "Hold your shepherd's staff over the water, and a path will open up before you through the sea." As you probably remember, God caused two huge walls of water to rise, and between them was a dry path, on which the Israelites hurried to the other side.

As soon as the last Hebrew was safe on the opposite shore, the walls of water crashed down on the Egyptians, who were still following them on the dry path between those walls of water. Every Egyptian soldier and his horse drowned, and with his chariot, were buried under the waters of the Red Sea (Exodus 14:5-31).

"When the people of Israel saw the mighty power that the Lord had displayed against the Egyptians, they feared the Lord and put their faith in him and his servant Moses" (Exodus 14:31).

…But how long would this last?!

Just ignore the little frog that hopped into the picture.

When Moses came down from Mount Sinai with the Ten Commandments in his hands, he was not aware that his face was radiant because he had spoken with the Lord (Exodus 34:29).

Obedience – Mission Impossible!

(Exodus 19:1-20:21; 24:1-18; 32:1-34:35)

Pharaoh and all of his army had drowned in the Red Sea, and the Israelites were now free from the threat of capture or massacre. Under God's direction, Moses continued leading Israel on their journey toward Canaan, the Promised Land. But this journey would take about 40 years because of Israel's disobedience and lack of faith in God.

About three months after the people of Israel left Egypt, they arrived in the desert of Sinai and set up camp in front of Mount Sinai. Soon, Moses went up the mountain to visit with God, who told him to say to the people:

"Now if you obey me and keep my covenant (the Old or Mosaic Covenant) then out of all nations you will be my treasured possession. Although the whole earth is mine, you will be for me a kingdom of priests and a holy nation..." (Exodus 19:5, 6).

When Moses returned to the people and told them what the Lord had said, the people responded together, *"We will do everything the Lord has said."* With that the Old Covenant was established between God and the people of Israel.

Moses then returned to the mountaintop and remained 40 days and nights with the Lord. During that time, he was given the tablets on which the commandments had been written by the very finger of God.

While Moses was on the mountain for this extended visit with God, the Israelites decided something had happened to him, and again they lost faith in Moses and in God. They talked Aaron into making a "visible god" that would continue leading them to Canaan. Since cows were sacred to the Egyptians, a golden calf was made from the Hebrews' melted-down jewelry.

The next morning, God saw wild dancing and revelry in the camp and told Moses what was happening. When Moses reached the camp and saw what was going on, he threw the tablets down, breaking them to pieces. Then he took the calf they had made and burned it in the fire, grinding it to powder. Moses then sprinkled the powder in water, and made the Israelites drink it. Other punishments were administered by both Moses and God.

God told Moses to chisel out two more stone tablets and come back up Mt. Sinai, where Moses stayed with God for another 40 days and nights. The Ten Commandments were again written on tablets to replace those Moses had broken. Other laws and ordinances were also given again, including God's instructions for building the tabernacle.

When God Tore the Curtain

When Moses came down from Mount Sinai with the two tablets in his hands, he was not aware that his face was radiant because he had spoken with the Lord. When Aaron and all the Israelites saw the radiance, they were afraid to come near him so Moses wore a veil over his face, which he would remove whenever he entered the presence of the Lord to speak with him.

What a special relationship God had with Moses! *"The Lord would speak to Moses face to face, as a man speaks with his friend"* (Exodus 33:11).

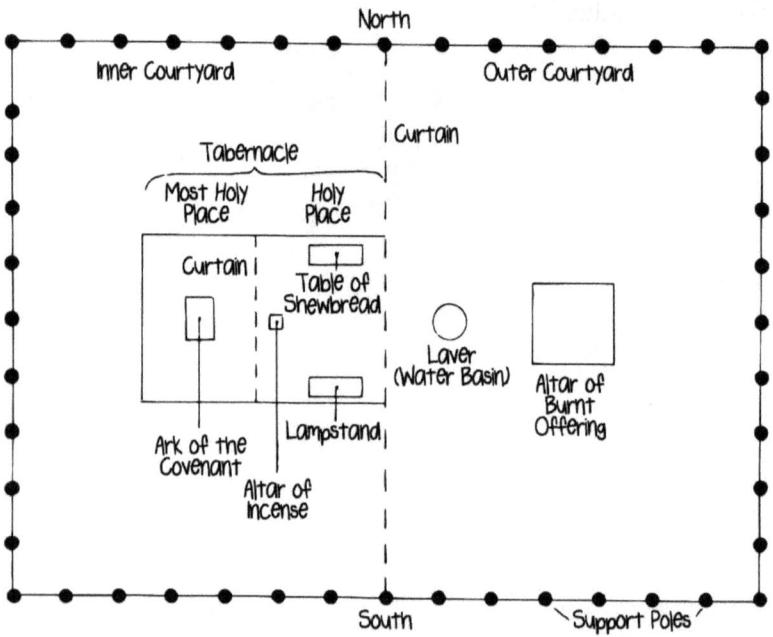

God was the architect for Israel's temporary tabernacle.
He gave Moses the building instructions on Mount Sinai.
(Exodus 25:8-27:21)

A Temporary Tabernacle and Priesthood
(Exodus 25:8-27:21; Numbers 17:1-11; Hebrews 9:1-10)

God was truly the architect for Israel's tabernacle. Instructions for its construction inside and outside were given to Moses when he met with God on Mount Sinai.

The **Holy Place** was in the east 30 feet of the tabernacle. It contained the **Table of Shewbread**, the **Candlestick**, and the **Altar of Incense**. Just beyond the Altar of Incense was a large curtain, or veil, made of the finest linen, which separated the **Holy Place** from the **Most Holy Place**, also called the **Holy of Holies**.

This room represented God's earthly dwelling place. The **Holy of Holies** contained only the **Ark of the Covenant**, which was a chest, 3 3/4 ft. long, 2 1/4 ft. wide, and 2 1/4 ft. high, made of acacia wood, overlaid with pure gold. It contained the two tablets on which were written the **Ten Commandments**, a **Pot of Manna**, and **Aaron's Rod**. (Numbers 17:1-12; 18:1-7).

Why was Aaron's Rod important?

There had been a rebellion among the Israelites concerning the selection of Aaron as the high priest. The Lord had commanded that a test be performed so that no one would again dispute the fact that he had chosen Aaron to be the high priest.

The Lord told Moses to get the staff from each leader of Israel's twelve tribes, to write the man's name on his staff, and then place the staffs in the "Tent of Meeting". "The staff of the man I have chosen will sprout," said the Lord.

The next day Moses found that Aaron's staff had not only sprouted, but had also budded and blossomed and was producing almonds... Case closed!

The high priest was the only person allowed to enter the Most Holy Place (or the **Holy of Holies**), and he could do this only once a year on the **Day of Atonement**. On that day, the ceremony was conducted for the forgiveness and casting away forever of all Israel's sins for that year.

The Priesthood under the Old Covenant

The priests were set apart by God to care for the tabernacle and later, for Jerusalem's temple. They were always from the tribe of Levi.

Aaron was the first High Priest. He and his sons and their descendants all served as priests. Other men from different families in the tribe of Levi served as assistants to the priests.

Hebrews 10:11 tells what it was like to be an Old Covenant priest.

Day after day every priest stands and performs his religious duties; again and again he offers the same sacrifices, which can never take away sins.

Animal sacrifices, ordained by God in the Old Covenant, were at the very heart of Israel's worship. This was God's *temporary* solution to the people's need for forgiveness and relief from their guilt. Even the Old Covenant was not put into effect without blood. *...and without the shedding of blood, there is no forgiveness* (Hebrews 9:22b).

The main ceremony for the forgiveness of Israel's sins was performed by the high priest once a year on the *Day of Atonement*. As mentioned earlier, the high priest was the only person who was permitted to enter God's earthly dwelling place, and he could do so *only* for this special ceremony. One bull and two goats were also part of the atonement ceremony.

The high priest offered the young bull to the Lord as his own sin offering to make atonement for himself and his household. He then entered God's earthly dwelling place through the **temple curtain** to sprinkle the blood of the bull on the mercy seat (on top of the **Ark**.) One goat was chosen by lot to serve as the sin offering for Israel, and the remaining goat was chosen as a "scapegoat."

After the high priest had confessed all of Israel's yearly sins over the scapegoat, he sent the goat into the desert in the care of a man appointed for the task. When they reached the desert, the man released the goat, which then disappeared, symbolic of the people's sins, never to be seen again.

But already, their sins were piling up for the next year's ceremony!

In the next chapter we will begin reading about Jesus, who became our High Priest for all eternity. Hebrews 10:12-14 tells us that **when this Priest (Jesus) had offered for all time one sacrifice for sins, he sat down at the right hand of God. Since that time he waits for his enemies to become his footstool, because by one sacrifice he has made perfect forever those who are being made holy."**

When God Tore the Curtain

Our Savior's first bed was a manger, a cow's feeding trough.

The time came for the Baby (Jesus) to be born, and Mary gave
birth to her firstborn, a son. She wrapped him in cloths and
placed him in a manger, because there was no room in the inn.
(Luke 2:6, 7)

Time for a Change - God Sends His Son

(Isaiah 9:6-7; Matthew 2:1-12; Luke 2:1-20;
John 1:1-4, 14; Philippians 2:6-11; 1 Peter 3:18)

In the beginning was the Word (Jesus),
and the Word was with God, and the Word was God.
He was with God in the beginning.
Through him all things were made;
without him nothing was made that has been made.
In him was life, and that life was the light of men
(John 1:1-4).

Early in the First Century A.D., a baby was born in a stable in Bethlehem. His bed was a manger, a cow's feeding trough. His mother was a young woman, probably still in her teens, and his first visitors were some poor shepherds, who had been watching their sheep in nearby pastures.

The birth of this baby had been prophesied for many centuries, and heavenly angels announced his arrival. From the beginning of time, the Lord Jesus had been working in the lives of the people he had created, but this was the world's "formal introduction" to Jesus Christ, the Son of God!

When God Tore the Curtain

For to us a Child is born, to us a Son is given,
and the government will be on his shoulders.
And he will be called Wonderful Counselor,
Mighty God, Everlasting Father, Prince of Peace
(Isaiah 9:6).

Even though Jesus is himself God, we are told that he was always pleased to do his Father's will.

(Jesus) being in very nature God,
did not consider equality with God
something to be grasped, but made himself nothing,
taking the very nature of a servant
being made in human likeness.
And being found in appearance as a man,
he humbled himself and became obedient to death –
even death on a cross!
Therefore God exalted him to the highest place
and gave him the name that is above every name,
that at the name of Jesus every knee should bow,
in heaven and on earth and under the earth,
and every tongue confess that Jesus is Lord,
to the glory of God the Father
(Philippians 2: 6-11).

There were three main reasons why it was necessary for Jesus to come and live, fully God and fully man, for about 33 years among the people he had always loved. All three reasons reveal this love for us.

Adam and Eve disobeyed God, and their sin nature has been inherited by every person from birth. Death is God's penalty for sin, and because Jesus is the only person who ever lived a perfect life, he is the only one who could die *in our place* for all sins – past, present and future.

Without Jesus, redemption by God would not have been possible. God's forgiveness would have been beyond our reach. And only because of the resurrection of Jesus, could every believer be given eternal life in him.

There were other reasons, too, why God sent Jesus. Under the Old (Mosaic) Covenant, most of Israel thought of God only as a stern judge without compassion.

But according to Colossians 1:15, *Jesus is the visible image of the invisible God...* For this reason, in knowing Jesus, people would know God's true nature - that he was not a vengeful God, filled with wrath toward his children, but a loving God, a loving Father, our Abba (Daddy) Father (Galatians 4:6).

As a *just* God, sin would be dealt with, but God's motivation would always be love for his children.

Some people who seemed to know Jesus well when he was living on earth still did not realize the connection between him and God the Father. Think about these words of Jesus to Philip, his disciple, recorded in John 14:9: *"Don't you know me, Philip, even after I have been with you such a long time? Anyone who has seen me has seen the Father... Don't you believe that I am in the Father, and the Father is in me? The words I say to you are not just my own. Rather, it is the Father, living in me, who is doing his work."*

Jesus ministered to people every day, sometimes through the twelve men he had chosen as his disciples. He taught in different ways: by his own example; by talking individually to those who needed special direction, comfort, and encouragement.

He taught groups of people in synagogues and homes, and sometimes *multitudes* of people on the mountainside and by the Sea of Galilee. Often he taught using parables about God and his kingdom, and about living lives on earth that honored God by serving others with love. Sometimes Jesus ministered through harsh words when situations required it.

Jesus healed all types of illnesses and afflictions, even bringing some people back to life from the dead. *He did only what the Father told him to do, and spoke only as the Father directed him to speak. He did nothing of his own will.*

We have barely touched on the third reason for the coming of Jesus. In the next chapter we will discuss the saddest day the world has ever known. *But even as Jesus was dying on the cross, God was revealing the importance of the third reason for his coming.*

The three main reasons Jesus came to earth:

1. Jesus came, fully God and fully man, to reveal the invisible God to mankind.

2. Jesus came to die for *all our sins* so that through his resurrection from the dead, God could give eternal life to all who would trust in him.

3. Having fulfilled the temporary *Old (Mosaic) Covenant* with his death on the cross, Jesus would become the permanent Mediator for the promised *New Covenant!*

These three steps would bring to light the glorious mystery "kept secret for ages and generations!"

When God Tore the Curtain

Why did God tear the curtain?
Was it because of anger? Was it because of sorrow?
No, It was the sign of something wonderful.

The curtain of the temple was torn in two from top to bottom.
(Mark 15:37, 38)

When God Tore the Curtain
(Mark 15:37-39; Luke 23:26-49; Hebrews 8:6-10:18)

It was 3 o'clock in the afternoon, but the sun had stopped shining three hours before. Everything was in total darkness and chaos.

The earth shook and rocks split. Some of the believers, who had died, came out of their tombs and were seen by many people in Jerusalem.

Just outside the city, soldiers on guard were trying to dispel the panic of those gathered on or near a hill named Golgotha (which means "the place of the skull"), but they themselves were terrified! Three men had been crucified and were still hanging on crosses for all to see.

In the temple something dramatic had also happened. God the Father, invisible but very much in evidence, had torn the heavy temple curtain in two, from top to bottom. Why did God do this? Was it because of anger? Or because of sorrow?

Hanging on the middle cross between two thieves, who were guilty of their crimes, was God's own Son, Jesus, who had lived a sinless life. He had been crucified for being God's Son and for bringing God's love to all people.

At 3:00 o'clock, Jesus called out, *"It is finished!"* He also called out to his Father, *"Into your hands I commit my Spirit."* That was the very moment God tore the curtain, which had separated the Most Holy Place, God's earthly dwelling place, from the rest of the temple. He had torn the curtain not because of anger or sorrow, but because of his love for you and me. God was introducing the **New Covenant.**

From the time of Moses until the crucifixion of Jesus Christ, the people of Israel had been governed by the Old (Mosaic) Covenant. This covenant had now been fulfilled by Jesus through his death on the cross *in our place.* All of our sins - past, present and future - had been forgiven forever by God! The temporary Old Covenant was now obsolete, and in its place was the *NEW COVENANT.*

Hebrews 10: 15-18 is a wonderful statement about this *New Covenant* mediated by the Lord Jesus:

"The Holy Spirit also testifies to us about this. First he says: This is the covenant I will make with them after that time," says the Lord. "I will put my laws in their hearts, and I will write them on their minds." Then he adds: "Their sins and lawless acts I will remember no more." And where these have been forgiven, there is no longer any sacrifice for sin.

The temple curtain separating God from his people was no longer necessary. *All people,* both Jews and Gentiles, could now approach our loving God at any time, in any place.

Through Jesus and his sacrifice, the sin issue had been taken care of once and for all, and the *New Covenant* had replaced the Old. But one step still remained in God's plan for all of his children, all of us who would trust in his Son Jesus as our Savior.

The moment you receive Christ, you receive His life and His total forgiveness, because both forgiveness and life are in Him.

What if there had been No Resurrection?

(Matthew 27:57-65; Luke 24:1-12; John 20:10-29;
Romans 8:9-11; 1 Corinthians 15:17-19)

When Jesus died on the cross for the forgiveness of our sins, he was setting the stage for his main gift of *eternal life.* But first it was necessary for Jesus himself to be resurrected from the dead.

Jesus lived a perfect life on earth, without sin. But if a good example was all he had offered or if the resurrection had not happened, his perfect life would not have mattered. As Paul said in 1 Corinthians 15:17: *"And if Christ had not been raised, your faith is futile; you are still in your sins."*

Jesus had died on the cross. There was no doubt that the Son of God was dead. The saddest day the world would ever experience had come and gone. But three days later, the world would witness a glorious miracle!

Very early that morning, Mary Magdalene had come with some other women to the borrowed tomb which had held the body of Jesus. They noticed that the stone had been rolled away from the entrance. When the women entered the empty tomb, two men in white told them Jesus had risen from the dead, just as he had told them before he died.

Mary left, but a little later she returned with the disciples, who still did not understand from the Scriptures that Jesus had to rise from the dead. The men soon went back to their homes, but Mary stood outside the tomb crying.

As she wept, she bent over to look in the tomb and saw the two angels seated where Jesus's body had been, one at the head and the other at the foot. They asked her, "Woman, why are you crying?"

"They have taken my Lord away," she said, "and I don't know where they have put Him." Then she turned around and saw Jesus standing there, but she did not realize it was Jesus. Thinking he was the gardener, she said, "Sir, if you have carried him away, tell me where you have put him, and I will get him.

Jesus said to her, "Mary." She turned toward him and called out in Aramaic, "Rabboni!" which means Teacher (Luke 24: 1-8; John 20:10-16).

That evening, Jesus appeared to his disciples, who were together with the doors locked for fear of the Jewish leaders. Jesus came and stood among them and said, "Peace be with you!" After he said this, he showed them his hands and his side. The disciples were overjoyed when they saw the Lord.

Thomas was not with the disciples when Jesus came, and he said to them, "Unless I see the nail marks in his hands, and put my finger where the nails were, and put my hand into his side, I will not believe it."

A week later, Thomas was with the disciples in the house. Though the doors were locked, Jesus came and stood among them and said "Peace be with you! Then he said to Thomas, "Put your finger here; see my hands. Reach out your hand and put it into my side. Stop doubting and believe."

Thomas said to him, "My Lord and my God!" Then Jesus said to him, "Because you have seen me, you have believed; blessed are those who have not seen and yet have believed" (John 20:19-29).

Jesus stayed on the earth 40 days after his resurrection, and during this time he appeared to over 500 people and taught them more about God and God's kingdom. He also performed more miraculous signs.

Where would you be if there had been no resurrection – if Jesus had not been raised to life after his death on the cross?

- Animal sacrifices would be your only means for obtaining forgiveness for sins and relief from guilt. And this solution would always be temporary.

- You would not be living under the New Covenant, mediated by Jesus, but under the Old Covenant in which disobedience meant death.

- And if you were not Jewish, the Old Covenant would not even apply to you.

- You would be praying desperately for a **New Covenant,** promised by God for *all* people.

- You would not have easy access to God. He would not be your personal, loving "Abba Father."

- If there had been no resurrection for Jesus, death would be final for you also. You would never experience the joy of eternal life in Jesus Christ!

When God Tore the Curtain

Letting God do his work through you
is a little like learning to float!

For it is God who works in you (through his Holy Spirit) to will
and to act according to his good purpose (Philippians 2:13).

WHO is the Holy Spirit?
(John 3:5-8; 14:16-17,26; 16:13-14; Acts 2:1-12;
Romans 8:9-11; Ephesians 1:13-14;)

God is a Trinity, or "Tri-unity." He is not three Gods, but **one God,** who reveals himself to us in three separate "Persons" - Father, Son, and Holy Spirit. These three Persons of our one God perform different roles in our lives, enabling God to work perfectly in every situation for our good and his glory.

For example, our Father sent his Son to become the Savior of the world. Then, when Jesus had risen from the dead and returned to heaven, the Father and Jesus sent the Holy Spirit to all believers to be their Counselor. But remember, God is one God. If the Spirit is in you, Jesus is in you. And if Jesus is in you, the Father is in you.

Jesus had talked to his disciples many times about the Holy Spirit. The night before he died on the cross, he said to them: *"I will ask the Father and he will give you another Counselor to be with you forever - the Spirit of Truth. The world cannot accept him, because it neither sees him or knows him; but you know him for he lives with you and in you"* (John 14:16, 17).

ARE YOU LIVING IN DEPENDENCE
ON THE HOLY SPIRIT?

Our problem is that even as Christians we still try to do things in our own strength instead of relying on Jesus through his Spirit in us. How do we turn complete control over to the Holy Spirit?

When you're swimming, do you sometimes enjoy just floating along on your back on top of the water? Or, when you try to float, do you start sinking like a lead balloon? Does floating look easy when others do it, but just plain impossible when you try it yourself?

Maybe you are relying on your own strength to hold you up, and that will never work! What's the key to floating? Lean back, relax, and trust the *water* to hold you up. All of a sudden you're ***FLOATING***!

In a similar way, when you lean completely on God and trust him to control your thoughts, words and actions through his Holy Spirit, you will be using God's perfect strength and not your own, which is always limited. Your life will have peace and purpose; and God's Spirit - the Spirit of Jesus - will never leave you.

You will be ministering to others with the wonderful Fruit of the Spirit: *love, joy, peace, patience, kindness, goodness, faithfulness, gentleness, and self-control* (Galatians 5:22-23).

WHAT IS PENTECOST?

The Holy Spirit first came to live in God's people 50 days after the resurrection of our Lord Jesus. Because the word Pentecost means "50th day", we call this special day the Day of Pentecost, and it marked the beginning of the Christian church. The age of the **New Covenant** was also fully launched.

It was such a thrilling day! As Jesus had instructed them, the Apostles were all together in one place. *"Suddenly, a sound like the blowing of a violent wind came from heaven and filled the whole house where they were sitting.*

They saw what seemed to be tongues of fire that separated and came to rest on each of them. All of them were filled with the Holy Spirit and began to speak in other tongues (languages), as the Spirit enabled them" (Acts 2:2-4).

People "from every nation under heaven" were also present. After hearing Peter's message in their own languages, about 3,000 trusted in Jesus and were baptized. Ever since that special Day of Pentecost, the Holy Spirit comes to live in each believer individually, the moment they trust in Jesus.

WHAT DOES THE HOLY SPIRIT MEAN TO YOU?

1. The Holy Spirit is your teacher, helper, guide, counselor and comforter. (John 14:16-17, 26; 16:13)

2. He seals your life forever in Christ. You never need to wonder if you will lose your salvation. (Ephesians 1:13-14)

3. The Holy Spirit never tries to "steal the spotlight." He exalts only Christ Jesus. (John 14:26)

If you have not yet crossed over to eternal life in Jesus,
would you like to do that now?

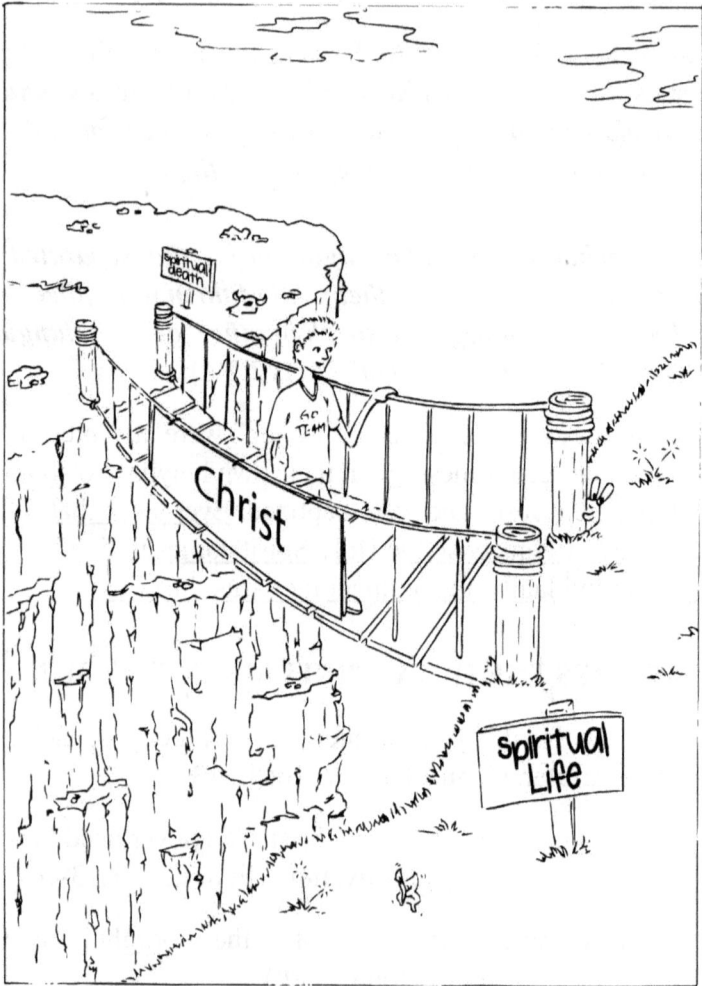

For God so loved the world that he gave his only Son, that
whoever believes in him shall not perish but have eternal life.
(John 3:16)

Have you Crossed Over to Eternal Life in Jesus?

(John 3:1-21; Galatians 2:20-21 Ephesians 2:8-9; Hebrews 11:6)

Jesus died on the cross *in your place* so that God could forgive you for all your sins – past, present and future. Three days later, Jesus was resurrected from the dead.

If you believe in Jesus and in his death, burial and resurrection, he will give you eternal life in him, beginning right now.

Your *faith* in Jesus is what saves you, but it helps to pray a prayer like this as a way of confirming this desire in your own heart:

Lord Jesus, I need you…

Thank you for loving me enough to die for my sins.

I know I will still sin sometimes,

but I know you died for those sins, too.

Thank you for offering me your life that lasts forever.

Please put your new life inside me right now.

I am so glad that you are my Savior now and forever!

Amen.

If you have truly trusted in Jesus, the living Christ has come to live in you forever through the Holy Spirit, and you have begun the great adventure for which you were created as a child of God.

You will still sin; and Satan, who uses a voice that sounds just like yours, will tell you that you couldn't be a Christian and do what you did. Don't you believe him! Jesus has already won the victory over Satan, and there's nothing Satan can do, and there's nothing *you* can do to pull you away from Jesus. All of us who have trusted in Jesus are safe forever in his arms!

Let us fix our eyes on Jesus, the author and perfecter of our faith, who for the joy set before him endured the cross, scorning its shame, and sat down at the right hand of the throne of God (Hebrews 12:2).

Because Jesus died *in your place,* and was resurrected from the dead, he has eternal life, and will never die again. Because you have trusted in Jesus – his death, burial, and resurrection – God has given you eternal life in him!

Jesus has done it all!

> *It is by grace you have been saved,*
> *through faith – and this not from yourselves,*
> *it is the gift of God – not by works,*
> *so that no one can boast*
> (Ephesians 2:8-9).

When God Tore the Curtain

You will always be under construction!

Therefore, if anyone is in Christ, he is a new creation, the old has gone, the new has come! (2 Corinthians 5:17)

Are You Ready for the Trip of a Lifetime?
(John 15:1-17; 2 Corinthians 5:17; Hebrews 3:12-15; 4:1; 9-11)

If you are a child of God through faith in Jesus Christ, he will invite you to travel with him to the NEW Promised Land. You will sail on "THE NEW COVENANT", and your Captain will be the HOLY SPIRIT.

How does it feel to be *ALIVE in Jesus?* You are a new creation, the *OLD* has gone; the *NEW* has come! (2 Corinthians 5:17) Are you ready to begin depending totally on Jesus to guide you in the wonderful life he has planned for you?

In an earlier chapter, we read that in the days of Moses, God had a Promised Land named Canaan for his people Israel. The *new* Promised Land, which he has prepared for you and for every believer in Jesus Christ is called *Sabbath Rest.*

You won't find *"Sabbath Rest"* on a map, but wherever you live, Jesus wants you to also live in *Sabbath Rest.* It is not an actual place; It's an *attitude* of trusting and resting in Jesus.

When you live in *Sabbath Rest,* Jesus will be guiding you through his Holy Spirit in everything you think and say and do.

If you leave **Sabbath Rest** for a while, you will want to return very soon, and Jesus will always welcome you back.

It's true that going to church every Sunday, reading your Bible and praying every day, memorizing Scripture verses, and being kind to every person are all things Jesus wants you to do. However, you still may not be *living* in **Sabbath Rest** – *not if you are doing these things in your own strength.*

Are you willing to stop trying to earn or merit God's love and forgiveness? You already have them! Put the **Old Covenant** aside *permanently*. It was only intended for Israel anyway. Now God wants you and all believers in Jesus Christ - Jews and Gentiles alike – to live life under his **New Covenant,** which he has provided for *all* people.

For many years, God had promised Israel that one day a **NEW COVENANT** would replace the Old Covenant, which God had always intended to be temporary. This day came when Jesus fulfilled the Old Covenant by dying on the cross *in our place* for all the sins of the world.

In the New Covenant, Jesus has only ONE command: *"Love each other as I have loved you... You did not choose me, but I chose you and appointed you to go and bear fruit - fruit that will last...This is my command: Love each other"* (John 15:12; 16-17).

God definitely wants us to share the love we have in Jesus with others – keeping this in mind, let us read *often* 1 Corinthians 13, the Apostle Paul's beautiful chapter describing God's perfect love.

AND NOW, MORE CLUES ABOUT THE MYSTERY THAT HAS BEEN KEPT HIDDEN...

The Old Covenant can show you that you have a problem and need help, but it cannot give you the help you need! **Today, the Old Covenant laws have one purpose only - to show you that you need a Savior.** God has provided a better covenant for his people: *for the law was given through Moses; grace and truth came through Jesus Christ* (John 1:17).

When you were dead in your sins and in the uncircumcision of your sinful nature, God made you alive with Christ. He forgave us all our sins, having canceled the written code (the Old Covenant), with its regulations, that was against us and that stood opposed to us; he took it away, nailing it to the cross (Colossians 2:13-14).

The prophet Jeremiah prophesied the coming of the New Covenant back in the 6th Century B.C. (Jeremiah 31:31-34). The Holy Spirit also testifies to us about the words of God concerning the New Covenant: *"I will put my laws in their hearts, and I will write them on their minds."*

Then he adds: *"Their sins and lawless acts I will remember no more. And where these have been forgiven, there is no longer any sacrifice for sin"* (Hebrews 10:15-18).

God had always known that the Old Covenant would be only a temporary solution to the needs of his people Israel. A better covenant was needed and would one day replace this temporary one for Jews and Gentiles alike. *The law was only a shadow of the good things that were coming - not the realities themselves. Today we can say with thankful hearts, "The Old has gone; the New has come!"*

Let us pray often for each other and be encouraged in our hearts by Paul's beautiful prayer about the love of Christ:

I pray that out of his glorious riches he may strengthen you with power through his Spirit in your inner being, so that Christ may dwell in your hearts through faith.

And I pray that you, being rooted and established in love, may have power, together with all the saints, to grasp how wide and long and high and deep is the love of Christ, and to know this love that surpasses knowledge – that you may be filled to the measure of all the fullness of God.

Now to him who is able to do immeasurably more than all we ask or imagine, according to his power that is at work within us, to him be glory in the church and in Christ Jesus throughout all generations, for ever and ever! Amen. (Ephesians 3:14-21.)

Dear Friend in Christ, May we rejoice more and more in the glorious *mystery* that has been unveiled through the *New Covenant:*

The mystery that has been kept hidden for ages and generations, but is now disclosed to the saints. To them God has chosen to make known among the Gentiles the glorious riches of this mystery, which is CHRIST IN YOU, THE HOPE OF GLORY!

(Colossians 1:26-27)

How do you picture God…

As a stern judge or a loving Father?

God: "I have loved you with an everlasting love.
I have drawn you with loving-kindness."

(Jeremiah 31:3)

God: "You will go out in joy and be led forth in peace..."

(Isaiah 55:12)

God: "Never will I leave you. Never will I forsake you."

(Hebrews 13:5)

God: "If you remain in me and my words remain in you,
ask whatever you wish, and it will be given you."

(John 15:7)

God: "Love each other as I have loved you."

(John 14:34)

God: "Don't be afraid; just believe."

(Mark 5:36)

*You received the Spirit of sonship.
And by him we cry, "Abba, Father."
(a term of tenderness, meaning "Daddy").
The Spirit himself testifies with our spirit
that we are God's children.*

(Romans 8:15-16)